What is cold?
Snow is cold.

What is cold?
Snowmen are cold.

What Is Cold?

by Lucy Lucero

SCHOLASTIC INC.

Photographs © 2012: Getty Images: 7 (Driendl Group/The Image Bank), 6 (Frederic Lucano), 3 (Jose Luis Pelaez), 2 (Mitchell Funk); iStockphoto/Kenneth C. Zirkel: cover; Media Bakery: 4 (Ariel Skelley), 5 (Ian Lishman), 8 (Trevor Lush); Shutterstock, Inc./Alexandra F.: 1.

ISBN 978-0-545-49720-6

Cover and interior designed by BHG Graphic Design. Photo research by Liza Charlesworth.

Copyright © 2012 by Lefty's Editorial Services. All rights reserved. Published by Scholastic Inc.
SCHOLASTIC, GUIDED SCIENCE READERS, and associated logos are trademarks and/or registered trademarks of Scholastic Inc.

12 11 10 9 8 7 6 5 4 3   18 19 20/0

Printed in China   68

First printing, September 2012

What is cold?
Winter is cold.

What is cold?
Snowballs are cold.

What is cold?
Icicles are cold.

What is cold?
Igloos are cold.

What is warm?
Mittens are warm.